Caged

by
Anna Imgrund

GLOBE FEARON
Pearson Learning Group

Project Editor: Brian Hawkes
Editorial Assistants: Jennifer Keezer, Jenna Thorsland
Editorial Development: ELHI Publishers, LLC
Art Supervision: Sharon Ferguson
Production Editor: Regina McAloney
Electronic Page Production: Debbie Childers
Manufacturing Supervisor: Mark Cirillo
Cover Design: Sharon Ferguson
Illustrator: Steven Cavallo

ISBN 0-130-23296-3
Printed in the United States of America

5 6 7 8 9 10 11   07 06 05 04 03 02

Globe Fearon

Pearson Learning Group

1-800-321-3106
www.pearsonlearning.com

Contents

1. Let's Rock

The lights go down. The building grows quiet. A feeling of electricity is in the air. And then, a voice cries out in the dark, "People of California! Men and women of L.A.! I give you the 'Animals of Hard Rock'! The boys with the big sound! The #1 rock group of the year! I give you — CAGE!"

With that, lights begin to circle left and right, and 30,000 excited people scream and make noises that sound like a small war. "Cruz Cage, Cruz Cage, Cruz Cage," the people call out. With a big smile Cruz Cage runs out as the screams in the building grow to a new high. Everyone else in the band is in place as Cruz picks up his guitar, throws out a fast "**1, 2, 1–2–3–4**," and leads them into their new Top 10 hit, "Falling."

Cruz looks out over the sea of people and works his guitar to the driving beat. A girl to his right is crying as she puts out her arms to him and calls out, "I love you, Cruz! I love you!" Another girl holds up a big white card that reads, "Marry me, Cruz!" The police are standing watch at all times, and from the corner of his eye Cruz sees one cop stop three girls and a short guy in a hat from running right up to the band! Without missing a beat, he goes on with his music and does not give those people another thought.

2. Looking Back

Raised by a young mom, Fannie Cage, Cruz Cage was born to the life of a rock star on the move. Sometimes he and his mom picked grapes for a living, and other times they headed down to the beach to hang out. One way or another, they were always moving around. It was a boyfriend of Fannie's who gave Cruz his first guitar. He stayed around just long enough to show Cruz how to play it.

Things might have stayed the same for Cruz if Fannie had not died the year he turned 15. After she died, Cruz packed up his guitar and walked or caught rides here and there for a while, not knowing what to do with himself. In the end, he had a feeling that the lights of the big city were calling his name. His last ride was with a truck driver who let him off at an L.A. bus stop late one night. From there, he walked to a run-down, hole-in-the-wall restaurant called Big Jake's.

It was Big Jake himself who told Cruz about a place called Cherokee House, where he could hang out for free. *Hmmm,* thought Cruz, having just put down his last $5 on dinner. *Sounds good to me!*

Every TV show and newspaper in the nation — in the **world** — knows what happened next in the life of Cruz Cage. The biggest show man in L.A. was talking to the head of Cherokee House and heard Cruz playing his guitar for the people who lived there. An introduction and two days later, history was made.

That man was Tyrone Miles. Some people thought he was nothing more than a shark, but he did help Cruz get a band together and put up some money to back them. *That's money I have given back to him many times over,* Cruz reminds himself often. Miles wanted Cruz to go right to the top. The only problem was, he didn't care what it took for Cruz to get there. Tyrone Miles was in it for the money, and he didn't care who he hurt to get there.

As Cruz plays his guitar before the people in front of him tonight, it seems that maybe, just maybe, he has lost a little of himself on the way to the top.

3. Cars and Stars

Cruz looks back at Mack, who is setting the beat with his sticks. Cruz points up, letting him know that this is the last song for the night. Mack shakes his head — *Got you, Cruz* — before the band lets go with a song from their new CD, "Leaving You." The people go mad! They scream! They cry! They pass out! *It just doesn't get any better than this,* thinks Cruz.

As the song comes to an end, Mack throws his sticks up into the air, and the band takes in the screams of 30,000 people.

"Can you believe it?" laughs Mack as they head back to the bus that is waiting for them. They can still hear the screaming people calling out, "More! More! More!"

"There were three girls who made it up the stairs before the police stopped them! Did you see them?" says Cruz. "I stood there thinking, 'Where are the cops? Where are the cops?'"

"And did you see that guy?" asks Ana, who sings backup. "The one the policeman took out?" She shakes her head. "I don't know — there was something about him that gave me a bad feeling."

There are 10 people in the band, and most of them get on the bus, but Mack and Cruz head to Mack's car parked close by. The next stop for the band will be an after-show dinner at Rhymes. "We'll meet you there," Mack and Cruz call out to the others. They get in the car with Mack driving and take off into the late California night.

Cruz puts his head back, closes his eyes, and starts to sing their last song of the night in a low voice.

"Hey!" Mack calls out at the corner light. "Was anyone else going to Rhymes by car?"

"No, I don't think so," Cruz says. "Why?"

"Someone back there is coming up fast and moving from one side of the street to the other."

"What kind of car is it?" Cruz wants to know.

"I can't tell," says Mack. "But it looks a little like a green FX-7."

"Just let him pass," says Cruz, his eyes still closed.

"That's the thing," says Mack, still keeping an eye on the car behind them. "He doesn't seem to want to pass."

Cruz turns around to look back, just as the driver in the car behind them makes his move. "This guy is out of his mind!" cries Cruz. "He's going to hit us, Mack!"

"Look out!" screams Cruz as the FX-7 hits them and throws their car into two oncoming cars. Mack tries not to hit the other cars, but he runs the car up on a sidewalk and through the glass window of a card shop.

Both Cruz and Mack are quiet for a little while after the car comes to a stop.

"Are you OK?" asks Cruz.

Mack's face looks white, but he says, "I'm all right."

"He's going to hit us, Mack!"

The two of them get out of the car and look it over. "Not pretty," says Cruz. "Not pretty at all." Now that he knows they are all right, Cruz tries to make a joke of it. "Of course," he adds, "it's not how I would have stopped a car, but I guess it worked."

"So next time," says Mack, his eyes on Cruz, "**you** drive."

4. Talking in Rhymes

Venus Standwell gets off the computer and puts her hands over her eyes. They hurt after too many hours on-line.

"You're not giving up already, are you?" asks Dan Nation, walking over to her.

"Don't kid me!" Venus laughs. "Do the words **Politics in the War of 1812** mean anything to you? I happen to know we are both working on the same paper," she smiles. "Can I help it if you're not as far along?" Venus, laughing, picks up her books and pulls her bag over her arm.

"When you're right, you're right," says Dan, taking over her computer.

"Even if you are a monster to say so, I might add."

"GRRRRRRRR," says Venus, sounding the part.

"Where are you headed?" asks Dan.

"Wouldn't you just know it?" says Venus. "I have to work at the restaurant tonight, which means I'll have to miss the 'Painting and Poems' showing. How about you?" she asks. "Are you going to be there?"

"I'll have to pass too," says Dan, pointing to the computer. "**Some** of us have homework."

"See you in class, then," she calls as she walks down the stairs and out of the building. She stops short outside the front door and looks at her watch. *Great,* she thinks. It's only 6:00, but night comes early this time of year. *What a good night to park in the far lot, Venus,* she says to herself, then shakes it off and starts walking.

By the time she gets to her car and drives to work, it's 6:30. *Dinner at Rhymes starts at 6:00,* she thinks. *Mr. Fields is going to kill me!* She pulls in a parking space and runs to the back door.

"Where have you been?" asks Mr. Fields, the owner of Rhymes.

"Sorry, Mr. Fields," says Venus, still running. "I was on-line at school, and the time got away from me." She gives him a big smile as she heads to her place at the front of the restaurant. "It won't happen again."

"It better not!" he answers, but he can't help smiling. Mr. Fields started Rhymes as a restaurant for writers, an offbeat place for people who love literature. And if ever there were a kid who loved the written word, it was Venus. He gave her a job last year — she was here all the time anyway — and she has become, hands down, his best worker.

Venus goes to the front door and tells Kay, who stayed late to work for her, that she can go. "You're great, Kay!" Venus adds. Kay waves as she walks away.

Rhymes is known as one of the hot restaurants in town, and Venus likes to think she has had a part in making it that way. The place is packed tonight, she sees, with more people coming in all the time. After she has seen the many people already sitting down, Venus sees a large group on its way in. She heads back to the front and looks to see who is doing the talking for the group. "How many will there be?" she asks the guy who looks like he's the boss.

That man, his strong face mostly hiding behind dark sunglasses, says, "I don't know. . . . Will you join us, pretty girl?"

Venus moves her eyes up to his and gives him a look that could kill.

"I don't think so," she says. "Now, how many?"

"Oooooo, you're losing it, big guy!" jokes one of the other men.

Not one who likes to be turned down, the first man tries again. "Come on, pretty girl, you can take a break long enough to sit with me, can't you? I'll make it worth your while!"

Venus cannot believe this guy. He will not take no for an answer! "Look," she says, "I am not your 'pretty girl,' and if you call me that one more time, the dinner you order will land on your head." She looks him right in the eye. "And if I wanted to sit down with you, I would. The answer, again, is no."

The eyes of the people around the man grow big, but he himself just smiles. "Miss," says one of his friends, "you don't understand. Do you know who he is?"

"No," smiles Venus, "**you** don't understand. I don't **care** who you are."

The group starts laughing, as if they need to let her in on a little secret. "This is Cruz Cage," says one guy at last, "and we are CAGE." He smiles as if that says it all.

"That's good," she says. "Now, let's try it one last time. How many?"

5. Down, But Not Out

Cruz sits in a back corner of Rhymes and watches Venus as she works. He finds it interesting that, once his group sits down, Venus does not even look his way again. He can't tell yet if that's good or bad, but it **is** interesting. He can't remember the last time any girl turned him down.

Work brings Venus back to Cruz's side of the room. He gives her his show-stopping smile, but it's no use. She doesn't even know he's alive. *Pretty girl?* he thinks. *What in the world made me say that?*

"What's eating you?" asks Mack. "Forget the girl! There are lots of fish in the sea, my man."

Mack is right, thinks Cruz. He tries to shake it all off, to think about all the other girls in the world who would give their right arm to be with him, but he can't.

Later, as the last of the food and drinks are taken away, she comes back. "I hope you all have had a good dinner tonight at Rhymes," she says. "Is there anything else we can do for you?" Venus asks.

"Yes," says Cruz. "Yes, there **is** something you can do for me."

Venus shakes her head. *Rich, good-looking, and without a thought in his head,* she says to herself. "And what would that be?" she asks in a cold voice.

"Will you just forgive me?" asks Cruz as the mouths of the guys at his table just about fall to the floor. "Forgive me for calling you 'pretty girl,' and tell me your real name." Mack shakes his head. He cannot believe it. *Cruz? Saying he's sorry?*

"Tell you what," says Venus. "Lose the sunglasses, and you're on."

Cruz puts a hand up to the glasses and pulls them off. No one else at the table says a word. Venus turns her head left, then right, looking at his eyes. You can tell a lot about people from their eyes, she knows, and she sees that his are bold, dark, and direct. "OK," she says. "I'm Venus."

"Venus?" says Cruz. "The planet?"

"No, the name," she says. "I'm Venus Standwell."

Venus, thinks Cruz. It seems right, somehow, for this girl full of fire and ice. "It's great to meet you, Venus," says Cruz. "I'm Cruz Cage, and these are my friends." He goes around the circle to introduce everyone.

"It's good to have you here," says Venus, "but I really need to go, so if there is nothing else—"

"But there is!" Cruz breaks in. Mack just looks at his friend. *Tonight, there is no telling what he will say*, thinks Mac. "When do you get off work?" Cruz asks. "We are going out on the town, and I'd like you to join us."

"Sorry," says Venus. "I'm off at 11:00, but I still have to study. Maybe another time."

"You're in school?" asks Cruz.

"Aren't you?" asks Venus. Everyone in his group seems to get a big laugh out of that question.

One fast, dirty look from Cruz stops the laughing. He turns back to Venus. "No," he says. "No, I'm not in school."

"Well, **I** am," says Venus, still upset by the laughs and the looks on the faces of the people with Cruz. It's like they have some big secret, and Venus isn't in on it. "So, if you don't mind, I need to get going," she says. "See you around."

You can count on it, Venus Standwell, thinks Cruz as he pulls his glasses back down and watches her walk to the front of the restaurant. *I'll be back.*

6. Hit!

Playing at 20 music halls in the next month means that it is some time before Cruz can get back to Rhymes. But the memory of Venus stays in his mind, and on his first night back in California, he heads for the restaurant. Through the glass of the restaurant's front doors, he can see her talking on the telephone.

"Hi," he says at last, walking in.

She puts the telephone down and looks up with a smile. "May I help you?"

I don't believe this, thinks Cage. It's been so long since he last talked with a girl who didn't know **everything** about him, from his middle name to the foods he likes to the songs he sings, that he doesn't know how to handle it. *What now?* he thinks.

"I — well, I was here before," Cruz gets out. "Remember me?"

Venus looks at him. "Oh, it's you," she raises her eyes. "Of course I remember — how could I forget a character like you?" She stands up. "I see you left your sunglasses at home this time," she laughs. "Good move. We keep the lights down in here," she jokes. "I think you're safe." She walks over to him. "Are you alone, or will others be coming?"

"I'm alone," says Cruz. "In fact, I was kind of hoping I could talk **you** into eating with me."

"Tell me," laughs Venus. "Why should I eat with anyone who calls me 'pretty girl'?"

"OK, OK, so I was wrong!" laughs Cruz. "How long are you going to hold it against me?"

"Forever," says Venus, " — and a day."

"So how about dinner?" asks Cruz.

"I can't," Venus answers. "I'm working."

"Tell your boss I'll make it up to him."

"What are you going to do?" asks Venus. "Buy everyone's dinner in Rhymes?"

"If I have to," Cruz comes back.

"Are you kidding?" she asks.

"No."

Venus gives him a long look. "Who **are** you?" she asks at a loss.

But before he can answer, a big circle of girls comes into the restaurant and gets a good look at him. *Oh, no!* He closes his eyes as he sees it coming.

"Is it you?" they ask. "Is it really **you**?"

"It's him!" one of them calls out. "It is! It's **Cruz Cage**! Hey, everybody, **it's Cruz Cage**!" And with that, Rhymes breaks out in screams and noise the likes of which it has never seen before.

Cruz looks over at Venus. The people have pushed her away as they run to get close to him. She falls to the floor after one of them pushes a little too hard. Cruz fights his way over to her and tries to help her up. "I'm sorry!" he calls out over the noise of the people. "I **did** try to tell you!"

But all Venus can say is: "You didn't try hard enough."

7. Rock's Not My Thing

Venus gets her bag from the back of the restaurant's kitchen, where Mr. Fields keeps it in a locked safe.

"Are you leaving now, Venus?" asks Mr. Fields.

"Yes, Mr. Fields," she says. "Everything is cleaned up out front, too, so you don't have to do it."

"Good job, Venus. Can you believe what happened here tonight?" Mr. Fields asks. "A rock star, of all things, at Rhymes!" Mr. Fields looks over at Venus as she waits by the door. "Did you know this Cruz Cage, Venus?"

"Yes and no," she says. "He was in last month with a group of his friends, but I had no idea who he was. In fact," Venus goes on, "I **still** don't know who he is. I'm not much of a hard rock girl, I guess. Oh, well," she says, "he's long gone now. See you later, Mr. Fields."

"You, too, Venus. Be careful."

Venus lets herself out the kitchen door and into the back parking lot. The night is a pretty one, and the air is cool, as winter is on its way. It is only as she comes around the corner to her car that she hears a sound and stops to listen. "Who's there?" she calls out.

"It's me," says a voice, followed by the sound of feet headed in her direction.

"Me who?" Venus, still scared, wants to know.

"If I called you 'pretty girl,' would that give it away?"

"Oh," she answers, seeing Cruz's face as he walks up. "It's you." She doesn't look too happy to see him.

"You don't have to sound so excited," he says, a little hurt.

"I'm not," she comes back. "Do you know how many problems we had because of you? Dishes on the floor, paper everywhere, drinks turned over — you name it, I cleaned it." She gets mad just thinking about it.

"I really am sorry," says Cruz. "But you're the one who told me to take off the sunglasses, remember?"

"Next time," she tells him, "don't listen to me."

"So there **will** be a next time?" he asks. "That's a start, anyway!"

"Don't count on it," she answers.

"Look," says Cruz. "I play in a band. That's what I do. I can't help it if people act that way when they see me! It's not like I ask them to. In a way," he adds, "I should be the one who's mad. You had never even heard of me!"

"Rock is not my thing," she says.

"What is?" Cruz asks.

"Literature," she answers. "Paintings, poems, good music —"

"And how do you know **my** music **isn't** good?" Cruz laughs. "Have you ever heard it?"

"Well, no," Venus says with a smile. "But I think I made a good guess."

"Let me ask you something, Venus," Cruz says. "You say you like literature, but does that keep you from reading other things?"

"Like what?" she asks.

"Like books on monsters, or love stories, or wars," he says.

"No," she says. "I read all kinds of things. Why?"

"Then, what makes you think that rock is all I can play?" Cruz asks.

"OK," says Venus, "you win. What else **can** you play?"

"That's the thing, see," says Cruz. "You'll just have to get to know me and find out!"

"And if I don't?" laughs Venus.

"Then I will come to Rhymes every weekend I'm in town," says Cruz, "**without** my sunglasses. That's a lot of drinks and dishes to clean," he adds.

Venus stops laughing and looks into Cruz's eyes. "I don't get it," she says. "Word has it that you could go out with any girl in the world. So why me?"

"Maybe," says Cruz, "there is just something different about you."

"And what would that be?" Venus asks.

"I don't know yet," he tells her, "but I'd like to find out."

Venus smiles. "That's not bad," she says. "Not bad at all."

"So you'll go out with me?" he asks. "I can learn to like literature if you will give rock a try."

"I don't know about that," she says, "but I'll get to know you a little, and we'll see how it goes." She looks around. "Where is your car?"

Cruz's face lights up as he walks with her to the street, where his car is parked. "Over here," he says, and they go toward the car, laughing.

Little do they know that they are not the only ones out on this cold night. Another set of eyes watches them as they walk through the lot.

I'll get him yet, the man says to himself, as he hides in the dark by the restaurant. "I may have missed on my first tries," he says in a mad voice, "but he will find out soon enough that no one— **no one**—gets the best of Spider Banks."

8. So Much for Fame

"Where are we going?" asks Venus as they drive away from Rhymes, not knowing that someone is watching every move they make.

"Wherever life takes us!" says Cruz. "How does that sound?"

"It sounds like a line you've used on every girl since you were a kid, if you ask me," Venus tells him.

"Not all of them," Cruz says, hurt.

"Look," says Venus, "I'm not some girl who is looking to get close to fame. If anything, your line of work is a turnoff. But I'll give it a try," she says. "Just be you, and I'll be me — OK?"

Cruz looks over at the ball of fire next to him. Never has a girl been so up-front with him. Never has a girl said what **she** wants to say, and not what she thinks **he** wants to hear.

"Really, where are we going?" Venus asks again.

"I thought we would go back to my place," says Cruz.

"No way," says Venus. "I don't even know you."

He pulls over and stops the car. "Where do **you** want to go?" he asks.

"How about a show?" she asks.

"I'd love to," says Cruz. "Problem is, the same thing that happened at Rhymes will happen everywhere I go."

"You mean people attack you that way all the time?" Venus can't believe it.

"I get used to it," Cruz tells her.

"So you can't go anywhere?" she asks.

"Not without fighting the ants."

"The ants?" Venus doesn't understand.

"The ants," Cruz says, "are what I call the people who follow me around trying to take my picture or get a news story."

"Where are they now?" she asks.

He laughs. "I make a game out of getting away from them. Sometimes I steal out the back door, and sometimes I lose them by driving fast. The main thing is just to lose them. But," he says sadly, "it's hard, and I don't always pull it off."

Venus listens as he talks. She had never thought about how hard it must be on someone who has fame. It always sounded exciting, but Cruz's life seems more like the plot of a bad book. "I know where we can go," she tells him, lighting up, "and no one will know you!"

"Where is that?" Cruz asks.

"It's a place called Fame and Fancy!"

"Next question," Cruz goes on. "**What** is that?"

"Just let me drive," she says, getting out of the car, "and I'll show you."

Never having let anyone else drive his $90,000 car, he doesn't know how to answer. But when she stands, waiting, at the driver's side door, he gives in. "It's all yours," he says, getting out with a smile.

9. Fame and Fancy

"What is this place?" asks Cruz, laughing.

"Fame and Fancy is a hangout like Rhymes," Venus tells him, "only everyone tries to come in looking like one of the big stars! See?" she goes on. "Everyone will just think you're some guy trying to **look** like Cruz Cage."

They sit down, and a girl comes over to take their order. "Good Cruz Cage get-up," she says. "One of the best I have seen, but the eyes are all wrong."

"I'll have to work a little on that," Cruz says, before he and Venus start laughing so hard that the girl leaves without taking their order.

"This was a great idea, Venus!" Cruz says when he can talk again. "I would never have thought of it!"

When the girl comes back again to take the orders, Venus asks for water and Cruz asks for a drink. Venus just looks at him.

"What did I do wrong?" he asks, picking up on her look.

"Do you really think you need that tonight?" she wants to know.

"You mean the drink?" he says. "Why not?"

"For one thing," she tells him, "it's bad for you. For another thing, it makes you do things you might not do without it. And I really don't like it."

This girl is different, Cruz thinks. "OK," he says, "if it means all that much to you, I'll go with water."

Her big smile is all he needs to tell him it was worth it.

10. Where Is the Quiet Life?

By the time they leave Fame and Fancy, Cruz knows that Venus is the kind of girl he could really fall for. Venus, on the other hand, is still not sold on the idea of going out with a rock star.

"But I'm a great guy, really I am," Cruz tells her with a smile.

She doesn't say so, but Venus has seen that much on her own. Cruz **is** a great guy. But she's seeing only a small part of who he is. It's the other side of his life she doesn't understand.

"Let's do this," says Cruz, "why don't you come with me when we play in Arizona on Saturday night?"

"I don't know," says Venus, getting into his car. "I don't want to hurt your feelings, but I'm just not into that kind of music."

"Will you think about it?" he asks.

"That I'll do," she tells him.

He closes her door and runs around to his side of the car, getting in to drive. They head back to Rhymes, where Venus left her car.

"Do you live here in town?" she asks as they drive.

"Sometimes," says Cruz. "My main house is here, but I have apartments and houses in other places too."

"Why?" Venus asks. "How many do you need?"

"I guess I only **need** one," he says, "but it's good to have other places to stay when you move around as much as I do."

"Then don't move so much," Venus says.

"It doesn't work that way," laughs Cruz. "And if I don't move around, then I get people camping by my front door as soon as word gets out that I'm in town."

"Camping?" she says. "In front of your house?"

Somehow, the way she says it, the life he has known no longer sounds like fun to Cruz. Being with Venus makes him want a more quiet life, a life in which he **can** take walks and go to shows and eat at restaurants without being attacked.

"What's wrong?" asks Venus. "You got quiet all of a sudden."

Cruz looks over at her caring face. "Just wanting what I can't have," he says sadly.

11. A Smashing Night

The lights are out in Rhymes as Cruz pulls up in the parking lot and drives to Venus's car. As he opens her door, she thinks the stars have never looked so pretty. *That has to mean something*, she thinks.

Cruz takes Venus's hand as they walk to her car, and they stand together under the night sky before she gets in.

"I really hope you'll think about going with me to Arizona on Saturday," says Cruz.

"I have to tell you that it doesn't look good," says Venus. "I have a paper to finish on top of everything else, and I'm running out of time."

"Do it on the way," say Cruz. "I'll get you a computer, books, whatever you need—just say you'll go."

Venus laughs. "I have to say, you **are** bold."

"I just know what I want," says Cruz.

Suddenly they both look up. They hear a high, machine-like scream coming from the other end of the street. Before they can get a handle on what it is, a car races into the Rhymes parking lot and heads right for them! Venus gets a look at the driver, a man, and sees that this is no accident. The man knows just what he's doing! He wants to hit them!

Cruz takes Venus's hand and the two start to run. But Venus knows there is no way they can outrun a car. "In here!" she screams, and pulls Cruz by the corner of a building, just as the car races by, missing them by no more than two feet. The car goes to the far end of the lot, then turns around.

"He's coming again!" she cries. "What now?"

Thinking fast, Venus throws her bag on the ground and looks for the passcard that will let her into the restaurant. "Here it is!" she screams. "Come on, Cruz!" They run for the door, and she passes the card over a light. The door unlocks just as he gets to them again, and they run inside just when—smash!—the car hits the side of the building!

"Here it is!" Venus screams. "Come on, Cruz!"

"Call 911!" cries Venus. "We have to get help!"

While Cruz runs to the telephone, Venus runs through Rhymes turning on lights right and left. "If he tries to come in to get us," she says in a voice of ice, "then we won't go down without a fight!"

12. After the Storm

"Are you all right, Miss Standwell?" asks the policeman.

"I—I think so," Venus says, taking a hot drink from Mr. Fields, but her hands are still shaking so badly that she sets it down.

"I'm happy you came in," Venus tells her boss. "But how did you know?"

"The police," says Mr. Fields. "They let me know that something was going on here at the restaurant after Mr. Cage's call came in, but I had no idea it had anything to do with you at the time. I'm happy I can help," he tells Venus, "even if it's only to give you guys hot drinks."

News people from all over the city are waiting outside the restaurant. Cruz Cage is big news, and a story about love, violence, **and** Cruz Cage is too good to pass up. "Do they have to be here?" asks Venus, closing her eyes against the noise and the lights.

Cruz comes over and puts his arm around her. "I'm sorry," he says. "I don't mind so much for myself, because I'm used to it, but I'd keep them from you if I could. The sad thing," he goes on, "is that they would leave you alone if it were not for me."

Venus smiles. "I guess I can take it if you can," she says.

"Miss Standwell," asks a policeman, walking over to them, "could you answer some questions for me?"

"I'll try," she says.

"Did you get a good look at the car's driver?"

"Yes, I did," she says. "There was a streetlight on, so I got a pretty good look." She shakes as she remembers. "I'll never forget it. He had a hat on, but I could still see that he had long, light hair and a round, fat face, and he looked like he might be short."

"What about the car?" the cop asks. "Did you see that?"

"I know it was green," she tells them.

Suddenly, Cruz remembers something. "Did you say it was green, Venus?"

"Yes."

"Could it have been an FX-7?"

"Maybe. Why?" she wants to know.

Cruz's face grows dark. "Because I think this guy may have tried to hit me before."

13. Spider Banks

The next day, Cruz and Venus are with the police again. "This lineup should not take long, Miss Standwell," they say. A policeman takes them into a dark room and points to a window on the other side of the room. Through the window, they see a group of men come out of a door and stand in a line, facing the window.

"Now, you don't have to be scared," a policeman says. "You can see them, but these men cannot see you. Get a close look. Do any of them look like the guy who tried to run you down?"

Venus looks at each of the men, but her eye stops at the one in the middle.

The policeman sees her stop to look at the one man. The policeman goes to the other room and orders the men to turn left. All the men turn to their left.

"Turn right," the policeman orders, and all the men turn right.

Venus points to the man in the middle. "That's him," she says in a bold voice. "There is no question about it."

"Just so we are all on the same page here, are you pointing to man #4?" asks the cop.

"Yes," Venus says. Already, her hands are starting to shake.

"Move to the front, #4," the policeman calls out. Venus suddenly pulls back into Cruz's arms as she sees a look of violence on the face of man #4, now that he knows he's been caught.

The policeman orders the men be taken away and asks Venus and Cruz to follow him to another room to talk.

"We thought that might be our guy," says the cop. "His name is Tom Banks, but he goes by the name 'Spider.' Do you know him, Mr. Cage?"

"I didn't know his face," Cruz tells him, "but it seems like I have heard the name. Let me think — Spider Banks. I know I have heard it somewhere."

"That's him," Venus says in a bold voice.

"Well, this may help," the policeman says. "We found these in his car." He sets down a big box, full of what looks like paper, in front of Cruz. As Cruz looks through it, however, he sees that it's not just paper at all! It's page after page of songs and music!

"**Now** I know where I have heard of this guy!" Cruz calls out, hitting his head with his open hand. "This is a guy who used to send us boxes and boxes of songs, poems, and music. He wanted us to buy them from him. We must have written him 100 letters telling him that we only use our own music and that we couldn't help him."

"Well," says the policeman, "he got your letters, and it looks as if he didn't like them much. Along with the box, we found these." From a bag, the policeman first pulls out a well-read Cruz Cage biography. Then he pulls out a paper showing directions to Cruz's home on one side and hand-written details about the star on the other. He next pulls out a hat, and Venus turns white. *It's the same hat!* Then the policeman puts his hand in the bag again. This time, when his hand comes out, he is holding a gun.

"A gun?" Venus cries out. "He had a gun?"

"Yes, he did," says the policeman. "He had two, in fact."

Cruz takes Venus, who is now shaking, into his arms. "It's OK, Venus," he tells her in a quiet voice. "They have him now. He can't hurt us anymore."

"I'm sorry," says the policeman, seeing that Venus is very scared. "You two can go. We just wanted you to know what we had found."

Cruz keeps his arm around Venus, and together, they walk out toward a car he has waiting. Mack is driving. Mack comes over to walk them out to the car. As soon as they are in the car and safe, Mack races away from the circles of news people trying to follow up on what will be the front-page story of every newspaper in America.

14. Mack Now, TV Later

Venus has never been so scared in her life. "He had two guns!" she cries. "Cruz, he could have killed us at Rhymes, at Fame and Fancy, in the parking lot — anywhere! And we never knew!"

"But he didn't," Cruz reminds her. "We are here, we are OK, and he's locked up."

"You have other people who want to get close to you. Any one of them might be just like Spider Banks!"

"No," he tells her, "they're not. Spider Banks was **not** a good guy, Venus. He was out to sell songs, and he was mad because CAGE wouldn't buy them! The people who really love CAGE are great," he goes on. "They may be hard to take sometimes, like when you're trying to eat dinner in a restaurant or go out with your girl," he smiles, "but it's because they like me, not because they want to hurt me."

"You think so?" asks Venus, feeling a little better for the first time since they found out about Spider Banks.

"I know so," answers Cruz. "I have lived with fame for a while. Now, I **am** careful, and I **do** have people working for me who watch out for me — but it's not because people are trying to hurt me all the time."

"Then where were those people last night?" Venus asks.

Cruz looks down. "The one part of being a 'star' that I have never gotten used to," he says, "is that I can't be on my own. I get sick of having everyone around me all the time. Last night," he looks up at Venus, "I wanted to be with you alone. Can you understand?"

"I guess I do," Venus tells him. "I **have** to understand, because that's what I wanted too. But, Cruz?"

"Yes?" he smiles.

"Next time, what do you say we let your people come along!"

"After all you have been through because of me," laughs Cruz, "I'm just happy there will **be** a next time. I don't care who comes along! The world can watch on TV!"

"Let's just start with Mack," laughs Venus. "I'm not ready for the world!"

15. A New Direction

The lights go down. The building grows quiet. That feeling of electricity is in the air. And suddenly, out of the dark, a voice cries out, "People of Arizona! Direct from L.A., I give you the 'Animals of Hard Rock,' the #1 rock group of the year! I give you — CAGE!"

And just as in California, Mississippi, D.C., Oklahoma, and the 1,000 other places CAGE has played, the people scream. They cry. They call out for Cruz Cage. They say his name over and over. But this time — for Cruz, anyway — things are different. Venus is here.

Cruz runs out with the band, picks up his guitar, and the rock sounds of CAGE go out to every corner of the building and bring the house down. They do "Falling," of course, and their back-to-back hits "B Cool" and "Top Dogs."

But then, with a little smile, Cruz Cage walks up to the front of the building.

"There is someone here tonight," he tells the people, his voice strong, "who means a lot to me. For her, I have written a song that's a little different from what you're used to hearing from us. But then, this girl is different too! I hope she likes my song," he goes on, "and I hope you all do too. I call it 'Venus.'" With that, CAGE takes it down from a hard rock sound to a slow, rich beat that makes everyone cry. And, as it ends, the people let Cruz know that this may be a good new direction for CAGE. They **love** the song!

Cruz comes down the stairs to Venus and puts his arms around her, smiling to see the happy look on her face. Together, they walk back up the stairs as more than 30,000 people show that they like both the girl and the song.

What great people! Venus thinks as she looks out over the big room. And, for the first time since Spider Banks ran them down, she feels that everything really **is** going to be all right.